The Klutz Book of
Inventions

HALL OF FAME EDITION

John Cassidy • Brendan Boyle

Table of Contents

How to Think Like an Inventor

Many years ago we at Klutz began our publishing enterprise with a how-to book on the art of juggling.

We didn't start the first lesson with a description of accurate throws or good catches; we started it with a step-by-step discussion of something we felt we knew a lot more about. We called it, "The Drop."

It's all about The Drop.

There's a reason for that, and it's not just because we're so lame. At Klutz — and IDEO Toy Lab — we're huge supporters of big flops and grand failures. Not so much because we enjoy the experience of a creative face-plant, but out of the belief that it's an absolutely necessary step. Potholes, dog doo, and unguarded edges are always on any path worth

**The wheel.
An early failure.**

The lightbulb is a particularly funny choice as the universal symbol of "sudden inspiration," since it took Edison years to get one to work. It is, for that reason, an excellent symbol of what the real process of invention is: a long road filled with failures, each of which steers the inventor on.

taking, and if you're not stepping into, onto, or over any of them — then the sad truth is, you're not going anywhere.

Nobody learns how to juggle without dropping a lot of balls and nobody invents anything very cool without making a lot of hysterically wrong turns.

Which brings us to this book, which seems to be about inventions, but is actually about something more — innovation, or how to think like an inventor. If you're interested in releasing your inner nutcase (which can often be used as another word for inventor), here's a thought exercise that we think will help.

Dignity is the enemy of invention.

Look at any common invention that we use every day. Start with the basics. The wheel. The fork. The modern nose hair trimmer. We guarantee that each of them was originally described as "ridiculous" and preceded by many, many failures. (The wheel looks like a no-brainer winner until you realize that there were no roads, no axles, no carts, and 6 zillion years of very successful living without one.) We don't know the real name of the person who invented the wheel but we're willing to guess what they called him behind his back — "Nitwit."

The fear of failure, of looking like a fool — in the eyes of other tribes or, more dangerously, in your own — is the single biggest obstacle to human progress in the history of history. If we could make one single change to human DNA, removing that fear gene would be it.

But in the meantime, we have a less surgical fix. We call it "play."

Most people will tell you that "play" and "work" are opposites. Work is serious; play is playful. Playful people are wasting time; serious people are doing productive work. But serious people are also concerned about the indignity of making mistakes, whereas fools wallow in them. And since progress is filled with mistakes, who are you going to call when you need some progress made?

Does this mean that Bozo should run NASA labs? No. But if the chief scientist at NASA doesn't push her researchers onto the thin ice of crazy ideas, her people and her results will be warm, dry, and boring.

The lesson here for any inventor-to-be is: Play with your problem. Do not be afraid. Go for lots of ideas, ridiculous to practical, and then go back looking for winners. Celebrate your mistakes, learn from them, and if people call you absolutely, 100%, no-question-about-it nuts… you're probably getting warm.

A funner plunger

The PogoPlunger

Who says clearing out a stopped-up toilet has to be a chore? With this idea, you'll look forward to every backup. Great for kids, adults, the whole family. Let everyone experience the joy of sewage with the PogoPlunger, the perfect marriage of plumbing and jumping.

Gives your pet a chance to contribute

The Wiener Cleaner

Dogs are like everybody else. They want to belong; they want to be a part of the family. But so often those feelings are frustrated by their sense of "differentness."

If your dog is troubled in this way, the Wiener Cleaner is just what the vet ordered. When chore time rolls around and the family is all there pulling together, strap a Wiener Cleaner on your little fellow, give him a chance to join the family, and watch his spirits soar.

Prescription sushi

Chopglasses

C hopglasses is an idea conceived at the (recently discovered) crossroads of European eyewear and Asian silverwear. On one end, stylish reading spectacles; on the other, easy-to-use bamboo chopsticks. Works as well for sushi as it does for small print.

High-Heel Training Wheels

Every girl remembers her first time in high heels. ("Finally growing up!") But too often the special moment is spoiled by an awkward stumble and crash resulting in embarrassing fractures and ugly contusions. There's nothing worse than finishing prom night at the ER.

What to do?

Take the high risk out of high fashion with high-heel training wheels. Sturdy, safe, and yet stylish.

Footwear goes ballistic

ShoeTers™

Are your feet cocked and loaded? When you jump up and down, do your enemies turn and fly? Do rockets chase them screaming down the street?

ShoeTers are just like ordinary shoes except they launch rockets whenever you jump up and down. The heels are specially made pumps that squirt powerful blasts of air that shoot rockets wherever you point your toes.

Relax and conch out
Ocean Ears

Here's the all-natural sleep solution for your next airplane trip. Instead of screaming babies, try the sound of soothing waves. Ocean ears consists of two conch shells on a headband that fit snugly over both ears. Slide them on (no batteries necessary) and listen to the sound of the ocean, not the engine.

You'll feel better.
And so will your flies.

Catch-and-Release Flyswatter

Being a fly is no fun. Garbage and dog doo aren't as tasty as you'd think, and your average fly would switch if he could. Also, most flies come from large families where the parents are emotionally absent and the little ones are left to fend for themselves at an early age. Given all that, it's no surprise that a fly's adolescent minutes are marked by long bouts of depression and paranoia.

Is there anything you can do to help?

Yes. Especially with the paranoia part. Our catch-and-release flyswatter relieves the flies in your life from at least one of their nagging issues — the possibility of instant violent death from above.

Of course, it's not just about the fly's feelings, either. Imagine what you'd think if you discovered that one of the flies you just smacked was less than five minutes old. Or perhaps a parent itself?

The catch-and-release flyswatter works just like a regular one except for the specially-designed spring-loaded trapdoor. Take your safely trapped flies outside and release them by the garbage cans. You'll feel better — and so will your flies.

Great on foggy days

Rolling Ball GPS System

The steering wheel-mounted rolling ball GPS system is a low-tech alternative to finicky, unreliable GPS units that require a Ph.D. in electronic engineering to understand. Each maze is custom-designed for your common destinations (school, work, store, etc.) and each snaps into and out of place in the center of your steering wheel.

To use, simply place the ball at "Home" when you're sitting in your driveway, and then start the car and turn the wheel to guide it through the maze. When you look up — presto! — you'll be there.

Dentist

ER

Grocery store

Preschool

*Patented rubber
butt-bladders do
the heavy lifting*

Inflatable
Booster Pants

Why are the people in front of you always so tall? Have you ever wondered about that? What are they? Zulu warriors? NBA stars? It's so reliable, it's practically eerie. Or maybe you were marked at birth. ("Please block my view. I was born to it…")

Fortunately, it doesn't matter anymore. With inflatable booster pants you can rise above them all. Here is how they work.

Squeeze the...

bulb to...

lift yourself...

higher.

The next time some giant sits in front of you, just squeeze the bulb on your booster pants. The built-in pump will add air to the sturdy rubber butt-bladders and lift you up. Guaranteed up to 16 inches of additional height. Beyond that, the risk of explosion is too high and you're off warranty.

Takes the guesswork out of ordering

Scratch 'n' Sniff Menus

Introducing scratch 'n' sniff menus, the "previews" of the restaurant world. With scratch 'n' sniff menus, the mystery meat will hold no mystery. Finally, you can order with confidence.

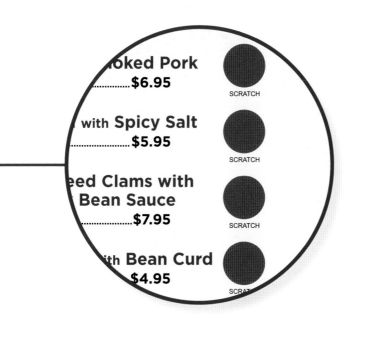

...oked Pork
...........$6.95
SCRATCH

with **Spicy Salt**
...................$5.95
SCRATCH

...ed Clams with
Bean Sauce
.................$7.95
SCRATCH

...th **Bean Curd**
$4.95
SCRAT...

Never run out of bathroom tissue again

Reminder
Toilet Paper

Are you always running out of toilet paper at crucial moments? Are you saddened when that happens? Or is "disappointed" a better word?

Either way, here's a foolproof invention for making sure it never happens again.

"Reminder" toilet paper is just like regular toilet paper except for the last four feet, when it gets different. *Really* different. That's when it turns into sandpaper.

You'll be amazed at the difference. And you'll be amazed at how well it stimulates your memory.

Your pencil-hunting days are over!

Pencil Lead Nail Polish

With pencil lead nail polish, you'll be carrying ten pencils with you at all times. No more frustration while you paw through drawers and under couch cushions. And bonus! Black is the new black. You'll be fashionable and functional, right down to your fingertips.

Helps develop early musical talent

Head-Mounted Drum

Everybody knows schools are cutting back on their budgets, especially in the arts, and that's why it's more important than ever for parents to step in and help youngsters develop their musical talents.

Which brings us to the head-mounted drum, a concerned parent's dream come true. Each drum is equipped with adjustable forehead straps, enabling it to mount firmly to the back of the head. Thanks to its convenient location, parents will be able to keep close tabs on their child's musical progress.

Comes with extra drumsticks in case of breakage.

Can't find your glasses? Not a problem…

Prescription Windshield

Here's a beautifully simple way to stop worrying about your glasses when you're driving the car. With a specially made prescription windshield, everything out there will be in perfect focus. For you. Which brings up the bonus! Once your car gets a customized windshield like this, you can stop worrying about anybody stealing it. Go ahead and leave the keys inside (right next to the barf bag).

Short
People
Hanger

Rearview relief

Rearview Mirror-Equipped Neck Brace

Anyone who's ever walked around with a stiff neck will appreciate the sheer relief built into this design. Two heavy-duty truck mirrors screw onto both sides of a standard neck brace. Result? No more blind spots. No more surprises from the rear.

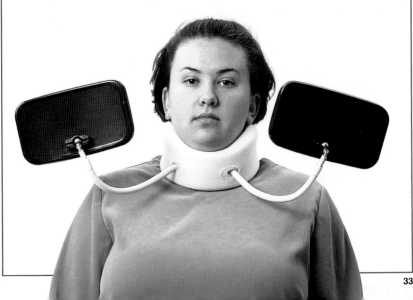

No frozen nose

Ear and Nose Muffs

Brrrr! Winter's chill is here! Fortunately, you're warm and nose-toasty with the world's first three-point set of ear and nose muffs. Each pair is made of fuzzy, warm, furlike material and designed to hit your comfort zone right on the nose.

What you can't see can't annoy you
Sibling Blinders

If you have a younger (or older) sibling, these blinders are designed to improve your view every time you have to ride in the backseat with him (or her). The comfortable headband means you can wear them just as well on endless road trips as on short trips to school or the store. Life just got a whole lot better.

Lighter-than-air mail

Helium
Bubble Wrap

Here's a handy way to cut your shipping and postage costs at the same time as you protect your stuff. Helium bubble wrap works just like regular bubble wrap except that the more you use, the less your box weighs.

The HeadBed

If you're a big multi-tasker (and let's face it, you wouldn't be reading this book if you weren't!), you'll appreciate the genius behind this idea. With a HeadBed on, you'll be able to attend meetings, or after-lunch classes, or just wait for the bus — and still get a nap in. It's a great way to squeeze two activities into the same time. Automatically doubles your productivity!

Puts wasted play energy to work

Lawnmowing Tricycle

Sure, you love to watch your kid having fun outside, but wouldn't you love it even more if he were learning some important lawn-care basics at the same time?

Of course you would. And with this three-wheeling lawnmower, that's exactly what he'll be doing. This tricycle comes equipped with a set of push-style lawnmower blades between the wheels. Your kid will love the extra challenge, and hey! He's out there pedaling around anyway! A win-win.

The scooter solution

Helmet-Mounted Rack

Convenience and comfort come together and sit right on top of your head in this simple scooter-friendly combo design. Put your books and lunch on the rack, hold them in place with the powerful spring, watch for low branches, and roll off to school.

Kiss toilet seat cooties good-bye

The Multi-Seat Family Model

It's hard to talk about good family hygiene these days without talking about toilet seat cooties at the same time. They're there. We all know it. Squirming around in their disgusting little microscopic ways. A big yuck. But what can you do about them?

Meet the multi-seat family model. A "concept commode" for the modern health-conscious family. Pictured here is the standard four-seater (Mom, Dad, Jenny and Charlie). But there's no reason the concept couldn't be extended up to five, six, even seven seats. Sure, you might need a little stepladder, but that's a small price to pay for the confidence of knowing that your seat was the only seat that your seat ever touched.

MOM DAD JENNY CHARLIE

Never lose your car in the parking lot again

Flip-Up Car Sign

A low-tech solution to an enormous modern problem. This high-gloss sign mounts on sturdy hardware on top of your car. When you're driving, it folds down flat. When you park — say, in the middle of some 40-acre, 6-million-car lot — just lift it up and lock it down. With its bright, eye-catching graphics,

you'll be able to see it from anywhere in the lot. So instead of wandering aimlessly around, you'll be able to look up and see your car, calling to you like an old friend.

Over Here Idiot

Sneezing in style
Sleenex Cuffs

When you're dealing with a nasty cold and runny nose, and a big sneeze is coming on, you don't have time to hunt around for a box of Kleenex®. Your needs are now. That's why Sleenex cuffs make so much sense. Each Sleenex cuff is a full-sized roll of tissue, designed to fit snugly around your wrist and stay right with you all day. It's an attractive accessory and a 50-foot-long runny nose rubber, all wrapped up in one.

50-foot Sleenex roll fits on wrist.

Finish that nap

Snooze-Equipped Smoke Alarm

Everyone knows how loud and annoying today's smoke alarms are, how disruptive they can be when you're on the phone or even when you're just trying to relax. It's a problem. But rather than curse the darkness, we decided to light a candle.

We took the standard smoke alarm design and added a key ("why-didn't-they-think-of-this-before?") feature: a snooze button. Now if the alarm goes off you can still finish your call or nap without having to deal with a lot of disruption.

Why should hamsters have all the fun?

Automatic Dog Walker

Dog walking doesn't have to be unproductive downtime. With this invention — a dual-tasker's dream machine — you can walk the dog at the same time as you watch TV or take a nap. The spinning wheel lets Biscuitbreath get his exercise while you hit the couch and grab a cold soda. A boon for anyone struggling to find enough time in the day to "do it all."

Thigh-Mounted Cup Holder

Swivels when you stand up.

For everyone out there who'd like an extra shot of convenience with their coffee, this is the invention you've been waiting for. The thigh-mounted cup holder keeps your beverages hot and handy or cold and convenient. And bonus! With its easy-rotate design, the thigh-mounted cup holder lets you sit or stand. Entirely up to you. Your drink is ready when you are.

Save dishwashing time

The Multi-Mug

Your coffee klatch is coming over this morning and you're starting to stress already. All that coffee. All those coffee mugs. And worst of all, all that dishwashing afterwards.

Wait! You've forgotten your new Multi-Mugs! You're a smart shopper and an environmentally aware one, too. By using Multi-Mugs you're able to cut your dishwashing water usage by two-thirds. And thanks to the unique equal-segment design, everybody gets their own favorite beverage. The lattes can live with the low-fats and everybody's happy. No backwash. No cooties.

Orange juice on the go

The Helmet Squeezer

Here's an invention that's all about just-in-time freshness: a specially-designed helmet with an orange juice squeezer mounted directly to the top. Just mash down on an orange and the juice feeds directly through the in-mouth tube. Wear it any time you need to combine cranium safety with tasty Florida refreshment.

*Put some real spice
in your life*

Shaker Ring

Jewelry and condiments come together in a fashion accessory that blends style and savor. Wear these attractive shaker rings and everywhere you go you'll be a little spicier.

Marshmallow Candle Cooker

Don't let the lack of a campfire stand between you and your marshmallow. This candle cooker is a handy portable alternative to messy, smoky campfires. Simple to operate and easy to clean, the candle cooker goes anywhere. To the office, car, class… anywhere the taste of a freshly toasted marshmallow would really hit the spot.

Watch a movie while you clear a forest

Chainsaw DVD

Chainsaws might be fine for cutting firewood or clearing out brush, but they're not very entertaining.

At least they didn't used to be!

Introducing the world's first custom-modified saw with a built-in DVD entertainment system. Going out to cut a trail will feel like going out to the drive-in. Pop in a new release, or maybe an old favorite, and catch a flick while you clear out a homestead.

REVENGE OF THE
SLIMERS

You'll be hoppin' bad
Pogo X-Treme

Better put your seatbacks and tray tables in an upright position, because we've just put the "go" back with the "po."

Turbocharged by a gasoline-powered scooter motor, this X-treme model is not your mama's 'stick. Designed for a new generation of thrill-seekers, this bad boy will clear a parked truck with more than ten feet of daylight. You won't believe it till you hit the ground.

Just pull up a chair

Reading Glasses

In the invention game, it's too often necessary to trade off form against function. It's tough to get both, and creating something that looks as good as it works is a needle that most inventors can't thread.

But we're not most inventors. Proof? These pull-chain-equipped, battery-powered reading glasses. In one stroke, we've hit the trifecta of form, function, and fashion.

"Get outta my way!"

Outboard-Powered Floaty

This concept-floaty is a new combination of old ideas: one, the proven excitement of inflatable pool toys, and two, the fun of wind-in-your-face powerboating. Put the two together and the result is raw, in-your-pool thrills. The outboard is a 12-horsepower 2-cycle engine, while the floaty is a real hot-rod rubber ducky, designed and rigged for speed more than comfort.

A sturdy rope (sold separately) enables the craft to double as a waterskiing towboat.

Soil it 'n' toilet

Flush 'n' Wash Baskets

These handy plastic baskets fit snugly into any standard toilet and hold up to six pairs of socks, three boxers, and two shirts. Put into place (lift the seat first, guys!), add soap, and hit the lever two or three times. Afterwards, a couple more to rinse and you're good to go. It'll be the cleanest thing you've ever taken out of your toilet.

Especially great for hotel travelers and apartment dwellers.

Fits all standard bowls.

Never miss an inning again!

Sporta-Potty™

The bases are full but so is your bladder. And you're sitting in the middle of a long row full of big people holding lots of nachos and drinks.

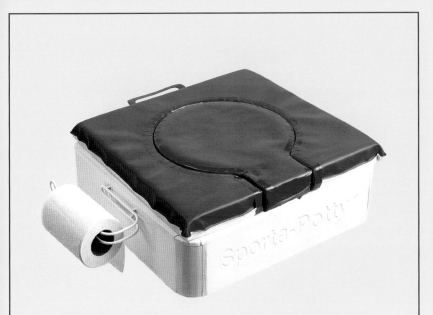

Not a problem. At least not if you're sitting on a Sporta-Potty, the world's first true, fully-featured, bathroom-equipped stadium seat.

The Sporta-Potty includes a soft cushion top, a handy cup holder, and most important of all, an internal, portable sealed-box "sanitary receptacle." Whenever you feel the need, flip up the top, expose the familiar seat, and you're good to go. Once your mission is accomplished, flip the seat back down and get right back to your game. With its unisex design, the Sporta-Potty works for both 👩 and 👨.

Cuts feeding time in half

Twins Spoon

This handy double-barreled spoon is a boon for the harried mom of twins. Puts efficiency back into feeding time. Two babies. One spoon. Genius.

What happens down there, stays down there

Soundproof Underwear

If your digestive process leads to the occasional embarrassing noise, then this could be an important innovation for you. What is it? Underpants that have been manufactured out of acoustic foam, a material specially designed to deaden sound.

Since it's made entirely from foam, soundproof underwear is obviously warm and comfortable, but its real virtue lies in its ability to kill uninvited noises. It knows (in other words) how to keep a secret.

Don't you hate it when people borrow your stuff?

Password-Protected Stapler

How many times have you come back to your desk and discovered a staple missing from your stapler? *And it's been moved, too.* Makes you spittin' mad, doesn't it? So then you put your name on the thing, in big block letters with the words "Property of" in front. And does that help?

We didn't think so. Fortunately, you've come to the right page. With our password-protected security stapler, you can rest easy, knowing your valued office supply is safe from thieving coworkers.

If you forget your password, go online, find the site that retrieves passwords, and look yours up.

Tasty Tees
SnackShirts

Each of these T (for "tasty") -shirts holds delicious fruit, drinks, or snacks. Bananas, colas, ice cream… all fit neatly into their custom-designed pockets.

Ice cream pocket

Drink pocket

The Human Roller Bag

This is an energy-saving two-part invention: coaster shoes on the feet, and an extend-a-handle frame on the back. Put on the shoes, get some sturdy person to grab the handle, lean back, and away you go.

Bring your own breeze
Sail Wagon

Here's the perfect way to set sail without going anywhere near the water. This innovative sail wagon design comes equipped with a 4-horsepower leaf blower mounted to the back.

KLUTZ

IDEO

All you need to do is hoist the sail, fire up the leaf blower, and you'll have a stiff breeze on your stern no matter the weather. Use the handle to chart your course and you'll be the captain of your own craft, master of your own destiny. Pack a lunch, weigh anchor, and cast your fate to (your own) wind.

Send us your invention.

Draw your invention and describe it, and drop it in the mailbox.

You've seen *our* inventions, now we want to see yours.

Come up with your own invention, draw a little sketch of it, and drop it in the mail to us. If it has that special blend of brilliance and deep dumbery that we seem to like so much, we'll include it in a future printing of this book, on the page that we've saved for you.

Deadline? What deadline? Our contests are never-ending. We'll just name new winners and switch inventions every time we reprint the book.

Our lawyer wants you to know: If your idea is really practical and will make you a million dollars, don't send it to us. Keep it and make your million. And then send us half since we were the ones who gave you the assignment. Any inventions that come to us go into a big public mix, so if you want them kept as your property or secret, please don't send them in, since they won't be after you do. By mailing them in, you are giving us permission to reprint them in future editions of this book, where everyone else will see them and probably make lots of money from them. Except not you.

Thanks, by the way.

Our lawyer

A never-ending contest

Here's our latest reader winner

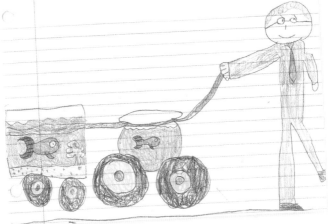

**Mobile Home for Fish
by Roberto, age 10,
Melvindale, MI**

"Instead of walking the dog, how about walking the fish? With this invention, you can bring your fish's mobile home wherever you go! If there is a pet contest, and the only pet is your fish, no problem! Also works with fish tank."

How We Did This Book

The 44 inventions described in this book came to these pages through many different doors. A few of them are old patents, at least one is a still-active patent, a couple of others are the brainchildren of contraptioneers (especially Rube Goldberg, Kenji Kawakami, André Montejorge, and Phillip Garner), but the vast majority came out of the bad dreams, brainstormers, and collaboration between designers, editors, and inventors at Klutz and IDEO Toy Lab.

The brainstorming process we used is one that IDEO Toy Lab has refined and perfected over the years, and it's one that actually has a firm(ish) structure, even though the outcomes are reliably unpredictable. A table is filled with people. Sugar, in some form, is provided. The rules of the game are painted on the wall.

The Rules to an IDEO Brainstormer	**The Ingredients**
1 Defer judgment.	
2 Go for quantity.	
3 Encourage wild ideas.	
4 One conversation at a time.	
5 Build on the ideas of others.	
6 Be visual. Use sticky-note sketches.	

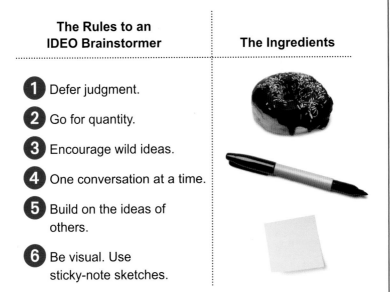

A challenge is written on the wall. It might be specific ("Blend two things. One, you bought at the hardware store. The other, at a gag shop"). Or, it might be more general ("Come up with a list of things that bug you in everyday life").

Markers and sticky notes are everywhere on the table and, for 5 minutes exactly, everyone fills sticky notes with single ideas ("A welcome mat crossed with a whoopee cushion" or "People try to make me eat vegetables"). At the 5-minute point, everyone puts down their marker and eats more sugar before starting another five-minute clock, and another pile of sticky notes is filled with the "mutts" that came out of the hardware store/gag shop matches, or solutions to the daily problems.

The Make-a-Mutt System

 **+**  **=**

Welcome mat   **Whoopie cushion**   **Whoopee mat**

In this way, you get a welcome mat that makes a farting noise or a picture of a clean plate you put over your vegetables.

We worked hard to make sure the brainstormers were goofy fun and we limited them to 60 minutes exactly, creating a comedy/sports atmosphere in which the opponent was the clock and the adrenaline of competition pumped it all up. Laughing was our success-o-meter.

The opponent

The Solve-a-Problem System

Vegetable horror   **Empty plate photo**   **The cover-up**

Last Step: The Group Build

The final step in the brainstorming process is the most important: the group build. Call it the "make it better" machine: One idea goes into the front end, a better idea comes out the back end.

Here's how it should go. Everyone presents their sticky notes to the group and puts them on the wall. Each of them is universally beloved since every idea is a point scored against the other team (the big bad clock).

Often, the sticky notes become the launching pad for further group discussion (the all-important "build"). This step — the most important one — goes a lot

Here's how we thought of the password protected stapler (page 80):

Everybody had to "buy" two things. One from a furniture store, one from a sports store. A lot of stickies were put on the wall, including this one.

BEAR TRAP ON CHAIR

"How about a snare on a stapler?"

"Make the chair actually work like a bear trap. A chair trap!"

"People are always stealing my stapler..."

"How about a bike lock or a stapler?"

"How about a mouse trap on a pen? A snapping pen trap."

Everybody started hollering changes. We ended up with .....

like a game of charades. Everybody hollers out random ideas, pushing the original idea in different directions. Nobody EVER says anything negative about any idea. The goal is always quantity ("We need MORE!") and the quality, remarkably, takes care of itself. We throw a lot of balls up and some of them, inevitably, go in. Here, for example, is how the group turned a bear trap on a chair into a password protected stapler.

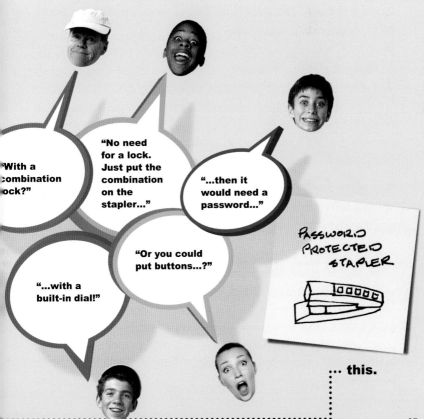

... this.

Who Did This Book

THE KLUTZ BOOK OF INVENTIONS is the result of a year-long collaboration between Klutz and IDEO, the legendary design and innovation firm. The Klutz team was led by John Cassidy and the IDEO Toy Lab team by Brendan Boyle.

Much of the collaboration took place in the form of brainstorming over lunch hours at the IDEO Toy Lab. Fueled by life-threatening dosages of pizza and doughnuts, zillions of ideas were fomented and eventually whittled down and refined into the 163 winners in the original *Klutz Book of Inventions*. From those masterpieces, we chose the 44 winners that you see here. The "invention-making" process that we used is based on one that IDEO developed, which we just described.

Both Klutz and IDEO Toy Lab are based in Palo Alto, CA, and share a firm belief in the powers of design and innovation and prototyping. And funny stuff.

Key members of the Klutz braintrust were David Avidor, Michael Sherman, Nicholas Berger, and Eleanor Hanson. Key members of the IDEO team were David Webster, Brian Witlin, Peter McDonald, Carly Geehr, Michelle Lee, and Miguel Cabra. Most of the ideas in this book were actually built in the IDEO prototype shop by Nathan Whipple and then photographed in action. For more information about Klutz or IDEO Toy Lab, please check out our websites.

Acknowledgments

Chief Inventioneers ...... John Cassidy, Brendan Boyle

Design........................... Kevin Plottner

Editor .... Pat Murphy

Photography .... Peter Fox, John Cassidy

Editorial Assistance ..... Rebekah Lovato, Dan Letchworth

Production Editor .... Madeleine Robins

Production..................... Mimi Oey, Kelly Shaffer, Linda Olbourne

Prototypes..................... Nathan Whipple, Joe Wilcox, Eleanor Hanson, Laura Torres, Charlotte Hutter-Brock

Acknowledgements and Inspiration

Philip Garner, Rube Goldberg, Kenji Kawakami, Annie Kutzscher, André Montejorge, Michael K. Proctor, Aya Tsukioka, University of Art and Design, Lausanne

Help and Contributors

David Avidor, Will Abbott, Edith Barr, Nicholas Berger, Dennis Boyle, Peter Bronk, Greg Brown, Tim Brown, Miguel Cabra, Paul Chaiken, April Chorba, Jim Collins, Brian Cook, Alex Coriano, Vicki Dalrymple, Andy Deakin, Kyle Doerksen, Elysa Fenenbock, Jim Feuhrer, Jessica Foley, Susan Fox, Carly Geehr, Adam Glazier, Derek Goodwin, Hans-Christoph Haenlein, Eleanor Hanson, Gerry Harris, Bladen Hawthornthwaite, Joani Ichiki, Anne Johnson, David Kelley, Tom Kelley, Vlasta Komorous-King, Kara Krumpe, Lauren Kutzscher, Michelle Lee, Gus Liu, Brian Mason, Gary Mcdonald, Peter McDonald, Nacho Mendez,Jaclyn Nolan, Woo Jin Park, Karen Phillips, Kevin Plottner, Mike Pollock, John Ravitch, Maria Redin, Dan Roddick, Diego Rodriguez, Michael Sherman, Jesse Silver, Mary Simon, Adam Skaates, Rochael Soper, Neil Stevenson, John Stoddard, David Strong, Joerg Student, Linden Tibbets, Ryan Traynor, Dorinda von Stroheim, David Webster, Erik Welker, Nathan Whipple, Joe Wilcox, Brian Witlin, Alison Wong

Models

Doug Analla, Kelly Ariagno, Andre Augustin Jr., Bandit Benson, Nicholas Berger, Scott Bryan, John Cassidy, Susan DeLance, Deja Delaney, Dewitt Durham, Bo Field, Franz, Sophia Hackworth, Chris Hadley, Zara Kestrel Harwell, Gary Hinze, Nina Hunt, Dick Kramer, Debra Lande, Gary Mcdonald, Colin Mills, Eric Mills, Mitchell, Eden Rose Murray, Pablo the Magnificent, Avi Runge, Josh Schneck, Emmett Stanley, Rick Tipton, Ryan Traynor, Sergio Valente, Erik Young, Lou Young

Art Credits

Page 1: Bowling ball © iStockphoto.com/NickyBlade. Page 26: Toilet paper holder © iStockphoto.com/kingvald. Page 32: Hanger © iStockphoto.com/skodonnell. Page 56: Jar © iStockphoto.com/winterling. Page 71: Floaty photo © ILP/Swimline – Edgewood NY. Page 74: Fans © Fotolia VI - Fotolia.com. Page 84: Girl © iStockphoto.com/perkmeup; Business Woman © iStockphoto.com/horrocks. Page 88: Lawyer © iStockphoto.com/fstop123. Page 91: Doughnut ©iStockphoto.com/ronen; Note © iStockphoto.com/bluestocking; Pen © iStockphoto.com/DNY59. Page 92: Whoopee cushion © iStockphoto.com/Joe_Potato; Welcome mat © iStockphoto.com/SAMIphoto; Page 93: Broccoli © iStockphoto.com/LauriPatterson; Plate © iStockphoto.com/bluestocking; Clock ©iStockphoto.com/Ridofranz.

The Outtakes

Remoteless TV

The Entertainmop

A great many things that we prepared for this book were cut as the editing process went on. Here are a few.

Combination Nose Hair Trimmer/BBQ Igniter

Swiss Army Broom/ Mop/Rake

Kitty Glitter

StayDry Surfboard

LED Bumper Stickers

Rubber Foot Dip

Powered Cotton Swab

Pepper grinder/ Baseball bat combo

High-Heel Skates

Edible Chopsticks

Toilet Seat/Scale Combo

Battery Charger Powered by Hamster Wheel

Parent/Teacher Secret Hypnotism Ring

Mosquito Attractant Spray (use on friends)

Lawnmower/Baby Stroller Combo

Adjustable High Heel

Gag Shop Parachute

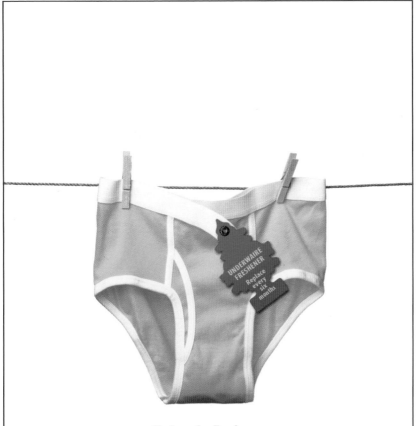

Underwaire Freshener

MAIL-IN REBATE

NOT PAYABLE AT RETAIL

TO RECEIVE YOUR MAIL-IN REBATE CHECK YOU MUST:

❶ Purchase ONE (1) new copy of the full version of *The Encyclopedia of Immaturity, The Encyclopedia of Immaturity Volume 2,* and/or *The Klutz Book of Inventions*. (This offer does not apply to the Scholastic Book Clubs editions of these books, to *The Encyclopedia of Immaturity — Short Attention Span Edition*, or to *The Klutz Book of Inventions — Hall of Fame Edition*.) You will receive a rebate of $3 for each qualifying title you buy.

❷ Mail your original register receipt for the above book(s) along with this completed rebate form (not a copy) to:

"The World According to Klutz Offer"
c/o Klutz, 450 Lambert Avenue
Palo Alto, CA 94306

NOTE: REBATE OFFER VALID ONLY ON PURCHASES MADE AFTER JULY 1, 2013,
AND ALL REBATE REQUESTS MUST BE POSTMARKED BY
DECEMBER 31, 2015 AND RECEIVED BY JANUARY 31, 2016.

Rebate check should be made payable to:

Name: _____

Address: _____

City: _____

State/Province/Territory: _____ Zip Code/Postal Code: _____

Email (optional): _____ U.S. Canada (circle one)

To receive the full $9 in rebates, you must buy one copy of each title.
What did you buy?

❏ *The Encyclopedia of Immaturity*
❏ *The Encyclopedia of Immaturity Volume 2*
❏ *The Klutz Book of Inventions*